BASIC / NOT BORING

SCIENCE
Grades K-1
Inventive Exercises to Sharpen Skills and Raise Achievement

Series Concept & Development
by Imogene Forte & Marjorie Frank
Exercises by Marjorie Frank

Incentive Publications, Inc.
Nashville, Tennessee

About the cover:
Bound resist, or tie dye, is the most ancient known method of
fabric surface design. The brilliance of the basic tie dye design
on this cover reflects the possibilities that emerge from the
mastery of basic skills.

Illustrated by Kathleen Bullock
Cover art by Mary Patricia Deprez, dba Tye Dye Mary®
Cover design by Marta Drayton, Joe Shibley, and W. Paul Nance
Edited by Anna Quinn

ISBN 0-86530-390-8

PRINTED IN THE UNITED STATES OF AMERICA

TABLE OF CONTENTS

Appendix

CELEBRATE BASIC SCIENCE SKILLS

Basic does not mean boring! There is certainly nothing dull about . . .
    . . . tracking animal tracks
    . . . taking a close-up look at some dinosaurs
    . . . finding the owners of fossils
    . . . unscrambling mixed-up zoo animals
    . . . seeing what air and water can do
    . . . getting friendly with bugs
    . . . figuring out if a rat can float
    . . . investigating a skeleton

The world of science is full of fascination for young children. This book is intended to capture some of that natural interest and use it to strengthen knowledge and skills. The idea of celebrating basic skills is just what it sounds like—enjoying the wonders of science while using and improving the skills that help to learn it. Each page that follows invites young learners to try a high-interest, visually attractive exercise that will sharpen one specific content skill. The skills are chosen to reinforce knowledge areas that kindergartners and first graders need to master. While students are polishing those basic skills, they're having fun investigating the world of science with Meg and Tom and their pets.

The book can be used in many ways:
* to review or practice a science skill with one student
* to sharpen a skill with a small or large group
* to stimulate a lesson that an adult will present to one or more students
* to assess how well a student has grasped a specific skill

Each page has simple written directions. It is intended that an adult be available to help students read the information on the page, if help is needed.

In most cases, the pages will best be used as a follow-up to a lesson or concept that has been taught. These are excellent tools for immediately reinforcing or assessing a student's understanding of the concept. In order for students to make the best use of the pages, provide them with resources and reference books, such as science texts, encyclopedias, and other science information.

As your students take on the challenges of these enticing adventures with science, they will grow! And as you watch them check off the basic science skills they've acquired or strengthened, you can celebrate with them.

The Skills Test

Use the skills test beginning on page 58 as a pretest and/or post-test. This will help you check the students' mastery of basic science skills and prepare them for success on achievement tests.

SKILLS CHECKLIST
SCIENCE, GRADES K-1

✔	SKILL	PAGE(S)
	Distinguish between living and nonliving things	10, 11
	Identify some parts of plants	12
	Recognize the life cycle of plants	13
	Identify some animal groups and their characteristics	14–16
	Describe some animal coverings	17
	Describe some animal movements	18
	Identify animal tracks	19
	Describe ways animals protect themselves	20
	Identify some animal homes	21
	Identify some animal habitats	22, 23
	Name some of the body's parts	24–27
	Identify some features of the skeletal system	25
	Identify the purpose of body systems	26
	Define and use body vocabulary	27
	Identify and describe the body's senses	28, 29
	Recognize healthy foods	30
	Identify and describe some ways to take care of your health	30–32
	Identify some safety behaviors and skills	33
	Describe the relationship of Earth, sun, and moon in space	34, 35
	Identify some planets and other objects in space	35, 38
	Identify characteristics of seasons	36, 37
	Describe some landforms on the Earth's surface	40, 41
	Describe some features of the Earth's oceans and waters	39–41
	Identify some dinosaurs	42
	Recognize fossils	43
	Identify and describe the three states of matter	44, 45
	Distinguish between solids, liquids, and gases	44, 45
	Describe and define some changes in matter	46
	Identify some properties of air	47, 48
	Identify some properties of water	49
	Identify some causes of pollution	50
	Describe kinds of precipitation and weather conditions	51
	Identify some pushing and pulling forces	52, 53
	Describe some properties of magnets	53
	Identify some uses of electricity	54

SCIENCE

Grades K-1

Skills Exercises

Is It Alive?

Meg and her pet, Rufus Rat, see living things all around them.

Plants and animals are living things. So are humans!

Living things need air, water, and food.

Living things make more things like them.

Color the things on this page that are alive.

Name _____

Use with page 11.

Life Characteristics

Basic Skills/Science K-1

Not Alive!

All living things need air, water, and food.

Living things grow.

Some of these things are not alive.

Color the things on this page that are not alive.

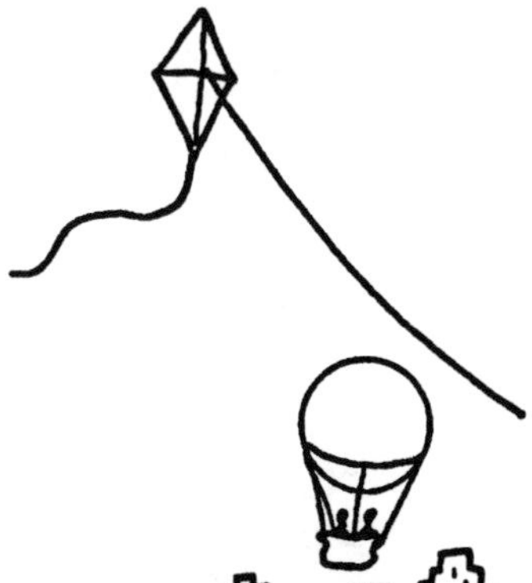

Name _____

Life Characteristics

What Good Are Plant Parts?

Meg's garden is full of plants.

Plants are living things.

Plants eat, drink, and breathe to stay alive.

Follow the directions to learn about the parts of a plant.

Leaves
help a plant make food.
Color the leaves light green.

Stems
hold up the leaves
and flowers.
Color the stems dark green.

Roots
hold the plants in the ground
and drink in water for the plant.
Color all the plant roots brown.

Flowers
make seeds.
The seeds grow new plants.
Color the flowers
any colors you like!

Name _____

Which Happened First?

Look at all the seeds Meg has planted in little plastic cups!

These seeds will grow into plants with leaves and flowers.

The flowers will make new seeds.

Then the plants will shrink and die and drop the seeds.

The seeds will grow into new plants!

This is called a **life cycle.**

Number the pictures in the order of the plant life cycle.

Name _____

Plant Life Cycles

Bugs in the Flower Bed

Rufus Rat thinks there are too many bugs in the garden.

Some of these bugs are insects and some are other kinds of bugs. **Insects** have 6 legs and 2 feelers.

Color the bugs in the garden that are insects.

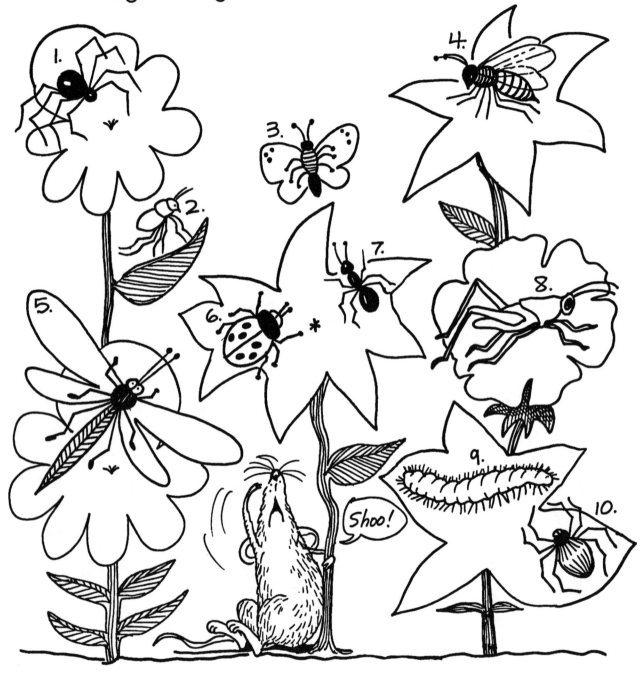

Name _____

Animal Classification

Copyright ©1998 by Incentive Publications, Inc., Nashville, TN.
Basic Skills/Science K-1

Going Buggy!

The bugs on the flowers are missing their legs!

They need you to draw legs for them.

The bugs with feelers are **insects.** Insects have 6 legs.

One bug is a **centipede.** Can you draw 70 legs on it?

The rest of the bugs are **spiders.** Draw 8 legs on the spiders.

Name _____

Mixed-up Zoo

Oh, no! Some of the zoo animals are in the wrong places!

Each zoo area has one or two animals that do not belong there.

Help Meg find these animals and get them with the right group.

Color each animal that is in the wrong place.

Draw a path for the animal back to the place where it belongs.

Name _____

Animal Classification
Copyright ©1998 by Incentive Publications, Inc., Nashville, TN.
Basic Skills/Science K-1

What Do Animals Wear?

Animals usually do not wear clothes.

Fur, feathers, hair, shells, and scales are the special coverings that animals wear instead of clothes.

There are different kinds of animal coverings.

1. Draw a green circle around the animal that wears scales.

2. Draw a red circle around the animal that wears a shell.

3. Draw a yellow circle around the animal that wears smooth, wet skin.

4. Color the animal that wears feathers.

5. Draw a blue circle around the animal that wears fur.

6. Draw a purple circle around the animal that wears hair.

Name _____

Animals on the Move

How does Meg's pony move? Does it . . .

run?   hop?   swim?   crawl?   fly?   walk?   climb?

Meg sees many different animals on her ride.

Each animal moves in a different way.

Write the word that tells how each animal moves.

1. _____

2. _____

3. _____

4. _____

5. _____

6. _____

Name _____

Animal Footprints

Animals and people leave footprints where they step.

These are called **tracks.**

Every kind of animal has a different track.

Draw a line to match the tracks with the right animals.

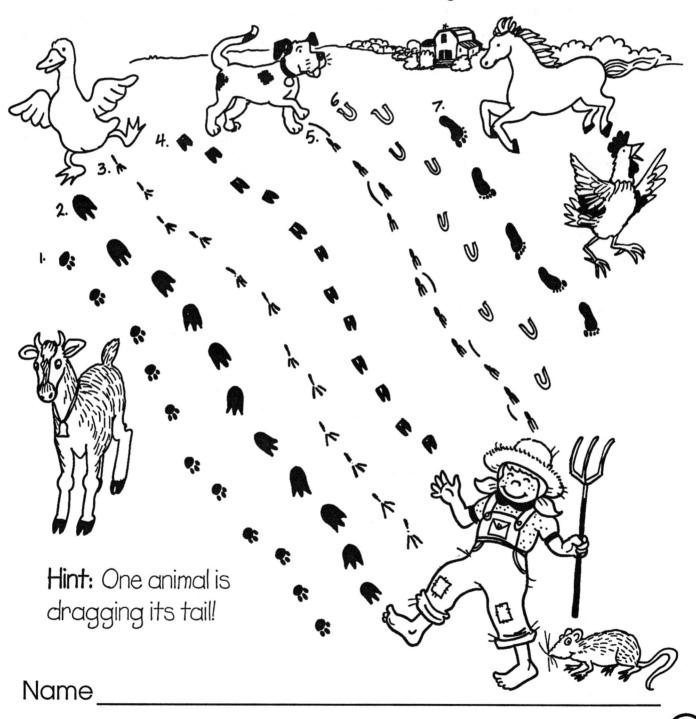

Hint: One animal is dragging its tail!

Name _____

Basic Skills/Science K-1

Danger!

Rufus has a trick to try to keep away from danger.

Other animals have ways to keep safe, too.

Match the words to the pictures of ways animals protect themselves.

Draw lines from the words to the pictures of the animals protecting themselves.

Where did that little rat go?

1.

3.

hide
run away
sting
make noise
warn

2.

4.

5.

Draw a picture of an animal running away.

Name _____

Something Is Wrong!

Meg has a great book of animal stickers.

Her silly pet, Rufus Rat, stuck most of the stickers on the wrong homes.

Color the animal that is in the right home.

Draw a line from the other animals to their real homes.

Name _____

Animal Homes

A Place to Belong

Every animal lives in a place with other plants and animals.
This is called a **habitat.**
There are many different kinds of habitats all over the world.
Help Meg figure out which habitat is right for the animals she drew.
Draw each of her animals into the right habitat on the next page.

A Place to Belong, cont.

Grassland

Desert

Rain Forest

Forest

Pond

Ocean

Arctic

Name _____

Use with page 22.

Animal Habitats

(23)

Body Parts You Can See

Meg and Tom are learning about body parts that they can see.

You can do the same thing!

Lie on a big piece of paper, and ask a friend to draw around your body.

Label each of these body parts on your body drawing.

head
hair

eyes
nose
mouth

shoulder
arm

wrist

hip
knee

leg

toes

ear
teeth
tongue
chin
neck
elbow
hand
fingers
belly button

ankle
foot

Tommy's Parts

Rufus
whiskers
ears
paws
tail

Name _____

Body Parts You Can't See

Tom has learned that the bones in his body make a skeleton.
Skeletons hold the body up and help it move.
Look at all the bones on Tom's skeleton chart.
Draw an arrow from each bone to the matching word.

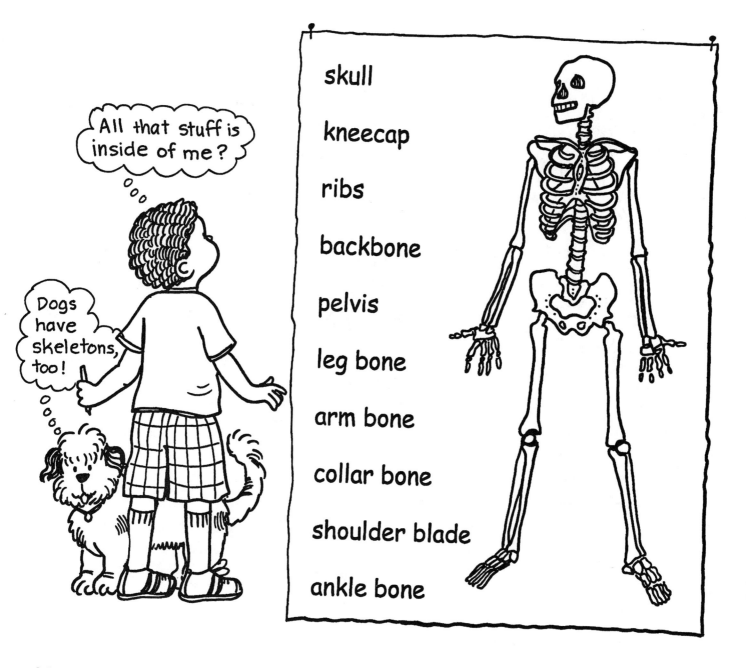

skull

kneecap

ribs

backbone

pelvis

leg bone

arm bone

collar bone

shoulder blade

ankle bone

Name _____

What an Amazing Body!

What amazing things a body can do!

Every human body has **systems** to do different things.

These words tell what some body systems do.

Match the pictures with the correct description.

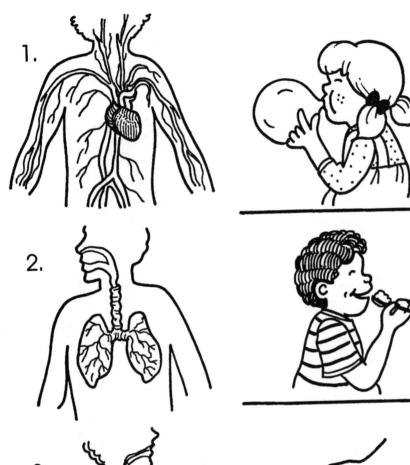

1.

The respiratory system helps people **breathe.**

2.

The digestive system **uses food.**

3.

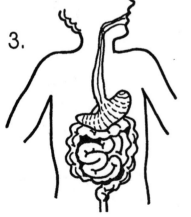

The circulatory system **moves blood** around.

Name _____

Body Talk

There are some words Meg and Tom need to know when they talk about the different parts of their bodies.

See if you know these words.

Write the word that matches each picture clue on the correct line of the puzzle.

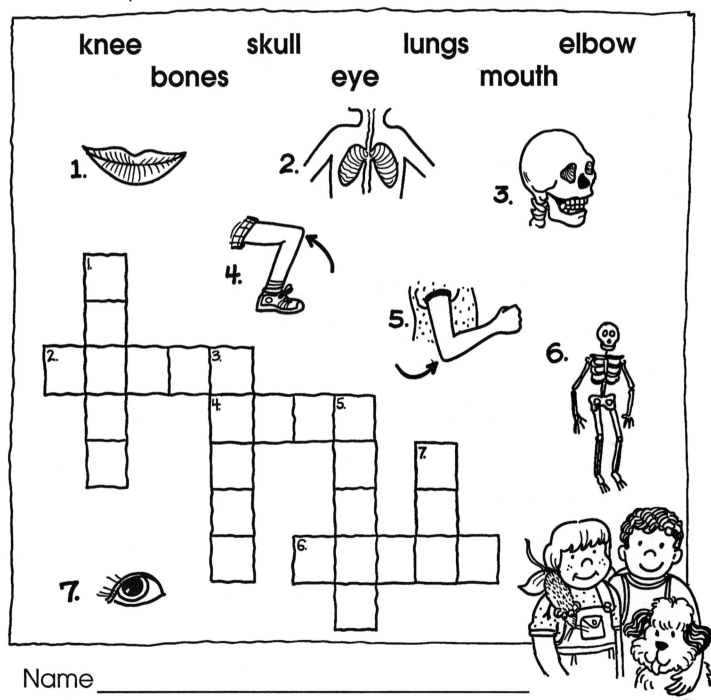

knee   skull   lungs   elbow
  bones   eye   mouth

Name _____

Body Vocabulary

Which Body Part?

You have five senses.

Each sense has a body part that helps it work.

Which body part is used for which sense?

Write the sense on the correct line. Use the words in the box.

1. _____

2. _____

3. _____

4. _____

5. _____

| see | hear | smell | taste | feel |

Name _____

Use Your Senses

Do Meg's ears help her enjoy her ice cream?

When she listens to music, does she use her nose?

Read each activity on the chart.

Put an **X** in the box if the sense is used in that activity.

Add two things to the chart that you did today.

		👁	👂	👃	👅	✋
○	1.	Eat ice cream					
○	2.	Play a drum					
○	3.	Scrape a knee					
○	4.	Take a bath					
○	5.	Listen to music					
○	6.	Hug a teddy bear					
○	7.						
○	8.						

sniff, sniff

Name _____

A Choosy Shopper

Which foods should Meg put in her shopping cart?

She wants healthy foods to eat.

Draw pictures in the shopping cart of six of the healthiest foods.

Name _____

Healthy Eating

Take Care

Meg, Tommy, and their pets all want to be healthy.

They do important things to take care of themselves.

Use words from the Word Box to finish the sentences that tell good ways to take care of yourself.

Word Box		
water	eat	sleep
clean	teeth	day

1. _____ healthy food.

2. Get lots of _____ .

3. Keep your body _____ .

4. Exercise every _____ .

5. Drink plenty of _____ .

6. Keep your _____ clean.

Name _____

Good Ideas

There are some great ideas on Meg's poster for keeping healthy.

Oops! There are some unhealthy ideas, too.

Color the pictures that show healthy things.

How many unhealthy things did you find? _____

Name _____

Healthy Habits

Basic Skills/Science K-1

More Good Ideas

Tom's poster is all about keeping safe.

He has shown some things that can be unsafe, too.

Put a big red **X** on the pictures that show unsafe things.

How many safe things did you find? _____

Name _____

Places in Space

Meg and Tom wish they could fly in a rocket and see planet Earth. Planet Earth is like a big ball moving around the sun.

The sun is a star, and it gives off light.

It is much bigger than Earth.

The moon is not a planet or a star.

It is a smaller ball that moves around the Earth.

1. _____

Label the sun, Earth, and moon.

Color the sun yellow.

Color the Earth blue and green.

Color the moon purple.

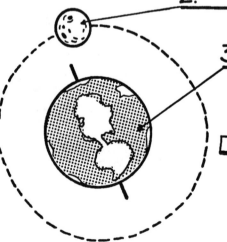

2. _____

3. _____

Name _____

Earth • Sun • Moon

The Spinning Earth

When it's dark, Meg looks at the sky through her telescope.

Do you know why darkness comes at the end of the day?

It is because the Earth spins.

The sun is a star that gives off light that shines on the Earth.

Where the sunlight touches the Earth, it is day.

Where the Earth is turned away from the sun, it is night.

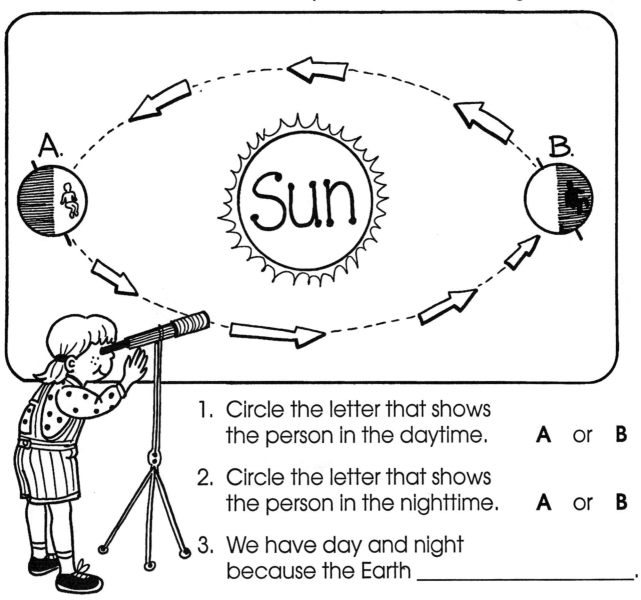

1. Circle the letter that shows the person in the daytime.   **A**   or   **B**

2. Circle the letter that shows the person in the nighttime.   **A**   or   **B**

3. We have day and night because the Earth _____.

Name _____

Day and Night

When Seasons Change

> What happens to plants in winter?
> What do animals do in spring?
> What is the weather like in summer?

When the seasons change, some things are different.

Draw pictures on the seasons chart.

Show some things that happen in different seasons.

Season	What is the weather?	What do animals do?	What do plants do?	What do I do?
summer	☀			
fall			🍂🌳	
winter		🐻		
spring				🪁

Name _____

Hot, Cold, or in Between?

The great thing about seasons is that the temperature changes!

Meg and Tom get to do different things in different seasons.

A **thermometer** tells how hot or cold the temperature is.

Use a red crayon to color in the temperature on each thermometer.

1. The temperature is 90° F.

2. The temperature is 60° F.

3. The temperature is 30° F.

4. The temperature is 70° F.

Name _____

What's out There?

Imagine Tom and Meg exploring in a spaceship!

When they look out their window, they see some amazing things.

Look at the words below.

Put the number of the word on the correct picture in outer space.

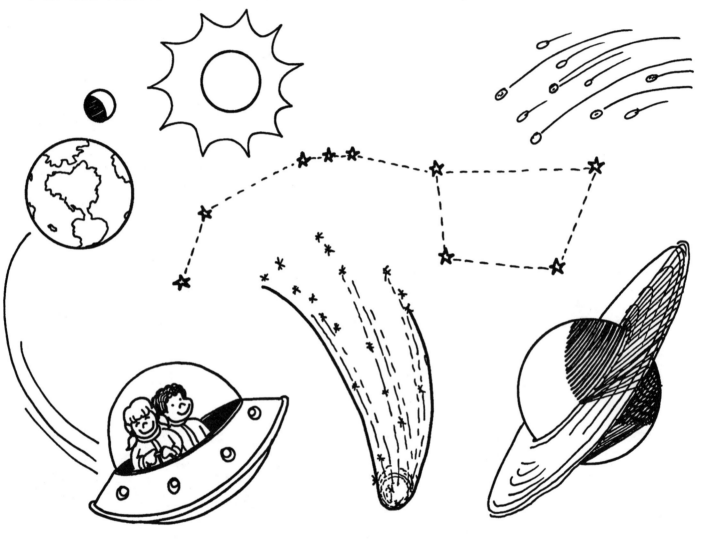

1. spaceship   **2. comet**   **3. sun**   **4. planet Earth**

5. the Big Dipper **6. shooting stars** **7. moon**   **8. planet Saturn**

Name _____

What You See in the Sea

The ocean is full of plants, animals, and other interesting things.

Lucky Tom is exploring the ocean.

Help him name some of the things he sees.

Draw lines to match the words with the correct pictures.

waves	shells	beach	kelp
octopus	fish	crab	island
diver	jellyfish	starfish	dolphin

Name _____

A Fish on the Hook

Do you know the difference between a river and a lake?

If you do, find the lake and draw a fish on Tom's hook.

Show what you know about Earth's land and water.

Draw these pictures on the map.

Name _____

A Fish on the Hook, cont.

...a palm tree on the island.

...flowers on the plain.

...trees on the mountain.

...a ship in the ocean.

Name _____

Use with page 40.

Basic Skills/Science K-1

Land and Water

Disappearing Dinosaurs

Learning about dinosaurs is a favorite hobby of Tom's. He likes the long names!

He knows that dinosaurs are extinct now, but a long time ago millions of them roamed the Earth.

Color each dinosaur the way you think it might have looked.

Triceratops lived in a herd for protection

Stenonychosaurus the smallest and smartest dinosaur

Brachiosaurus the biggest dinosaur

Tyrannosaurus Rex the meanest dinosaur

Stegosaurus the dinosaur with the smallest brain

Name _____

Old Bones and Fossils

How do scientists know what dinosaurs looked like?

They study old bones and put them together.

These old bones are **fossils.**

Draw a line to match each fossil with the thing that made it.

A **fossil** is a print or a part of a plant or animal that lived long ago.

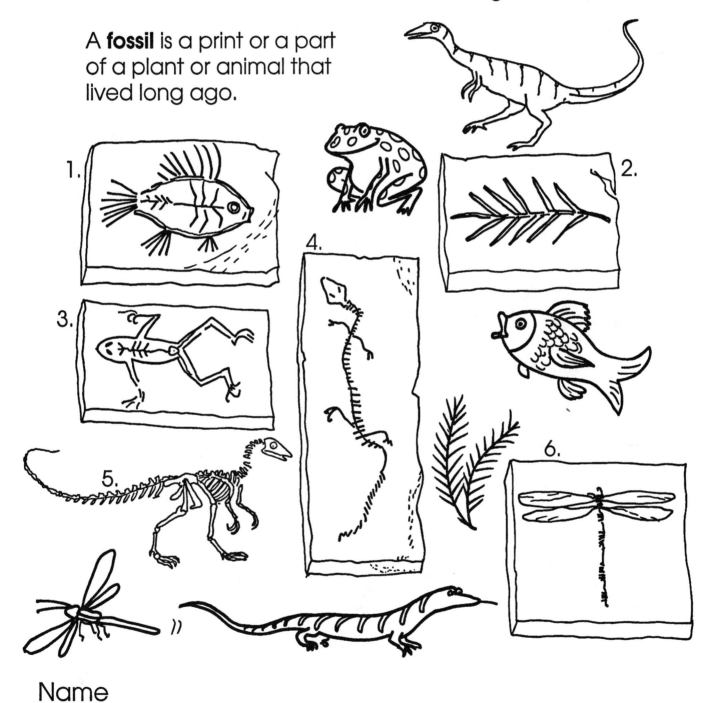

Name _____

Fossils

Three Kinds of Matter

All the things in the world are called **matter.**

Which kind of matter is down below Meg and Aunt Betty?

A **solid** has shape and size.

A **liquid** has a size, but no shape.

A liquid changes shape to fit its container.

Liquids can pour.

A **gas** has no size and no shape.

A gas takes the size and shape of its container.

Finish the chart to show what kind of matter each thing is.

	Solid	Liquid	Gas
1. 			
2.			
3.			
4.			
5.			
6.			

Name _____

Forms of Matter

Basic Skills/Science K-1

Solid or Liquid?

Today, Tom really has his hands full!

He is trying to give Tipper a bath, but it is not an easy job!

Find the solids in the picture. Color them **red.**

Find the liquids. Color them **blue.**

A **solid** has shape and size.

A **liquid** has a size,
but no shape.
A liquid changes shape.
Liquids can pour.

Cola

Flea Powder

Shampoo

Name _____

Things Are Changing

Meg is changing. She is a year older today! Look for other changes happening at Meg's party.

Write the correct word from the **Word Box** beside each number to show the cause of the change.

Word Box		
bake	burn	melt
boil	freeze	mix
	expand	

1. _____

2. _____

3. _____

4. _____

5. _____

6. _____

7. _____

Name _____

Changes in Matter

Basic Skills/Science K-1

Oh! What Air Can Do!

The balloons at Meg's party are full of air!
Air is everywhere! Air moves things!
Air fills things up! We breathe air.

The pictures show some things that air can do.
Draw two pictures of other things air can do.

1.

2.

3.

4.

5.

Name _____

Air Properties

How Much Air?

Air is made of different gases.
Air takes up space.
Air does not have its own
shape or size.

Which has more air. . .
a full tire or a flat tire?

In each row, color the thing that has the most air.

help !

Name _____

Happy Floating

Rufus Rat is happy because he can float.

Fill a dishpan or sink with water.

Try to float each of these things.

Think of some other things to try to float.

Circle **yes** or **no** to show which things will float.

1. rubber ball

yes   no

2. sponge

yes   no

3. paper

yes   no

4. plastic spoon

yes   no

5. rock

yes   no

6. paper clip

yes   no

7. empty jar with top

yes

no

Name _____

X out Pollution

All living things—including Tom and Meg—need clean, fresh air.

Unclean air causes them to be unhealthy.

Unclean air is called **polluted air.**

Make an **X** on the things that cause air pollution.

Name _____

Which Weather?

Rufus Rat needs your help.

He needs to know the names of each type of weather.

Draw a line from each picture to the right
weather word.

hail	rain	wind	thunder-storm
sunshine	snow	tornado	clouds

Name _____

Pushing and Pulling

There's a lot of pulling going on in this Tug-of-War.

Nothing can begin to move unless something pushes or pulls it.

A push or pull is called a **force.**

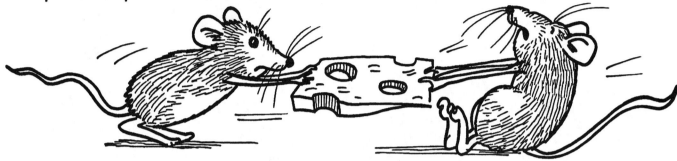

Draw an arrow to point at the force in each picture.

Circle the animal that needs more force to get moving.

Name _____

A Big Attraction

Get a magnet, and collect these things.
Try to attract each one.
Does the magnet attract it? Circle **yes** or **no.**

1. plastic glass
yes   no

2. rubber ball
yes   no

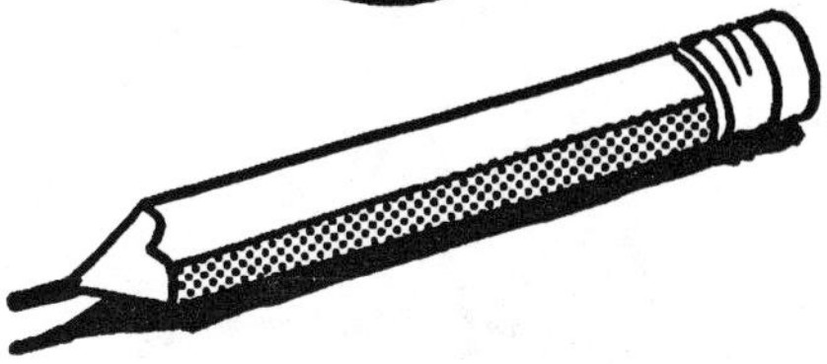

3. thumbtacks
yes   no

4. pencil
yes   no

5. cracker
yes   no

6. paper clip
yes   no

7. scissors
yes   no

8. plastic spoon
yes   no

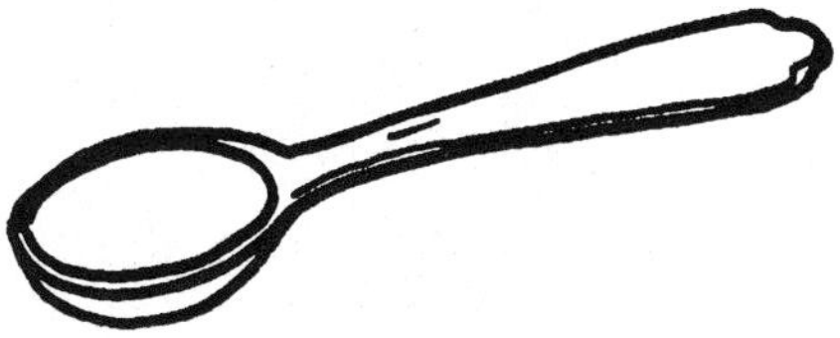

Name _____

Magnets

Scrambled Pictures

Electricity is a big word. Electricity makes many things work.

Look at the scrambled pictures.

Some things that use electricity are in this picture. Find them.

Trace the outline in red if the object uses electricity.

Trace the outline in blue if the object doesn't use electricity.

How many things that use electricity did you find? _____

Name _____

Science Words to Know

air: Air is a gas. All living things need it.

astronaut: An astronaut is a person who travels and works in space.

attract: Magnets attract some things made of metal.

body covering: The body covering is what covers a body. A bird's body covering is feathers.

bones: Bones are hard substances that support your body. Your skeleton is made of bones.

dinosaur: Dinosaurs are reptiles that do not live on Earth anymore.

Earth: Earth is the planet where we live.

electricity: Electricity is a kind of power. A stove uses electricity to cook things.

evaporation: Evaporation happens when a liquid changes into a gas. Water evaporates into the air.

exercise: You exercise when you move your body. Exercise keeps your body strong and healthy.

fossil: A fossil is a print of a plant or animal that lived long ago.

float: A boat can float on water.

flower: A flower is a plant with petals that makes seeds.

force: A force is a push or pull.

gas: A gas has no size or shape.

habitat: A habitat is the area where something lives. The bird's habitat takes care of its needs.

heart: The heart is the part of the body that pumps blood through the body.

home: A home is where an animal lives. The tree is home to these birds.

island: An island is land that has water all around it.

leaves: Leaves are a part of a plant that help it make food.

liquid: A liquid has size but no shape. A liquid can pour.

living things: Animals and plants are living things.

lungs: Lungs are a part of your body that help you breathe.

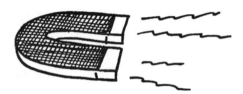

magnet: A magnet attracts some metal things.

moon: The moon is a round body that travels around the Earth.

muscles: Muscles help your body move.

ocean: An ocean is a large body of salt water. Many plants and animals live in the ocean.

planet: A planet is a body in outer space that spins around a star. Earth travels around the sun.

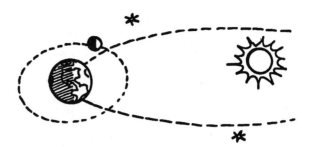

roots: The roots of a plant drink water.

seasons: Seasons are the four times of the year: summer, fall, winter, and spring.

seeds: Seeds can grow into plants.

senses: Senses help you see, feel, hear, taste, and smell.

shadow: Shadows are made when the sun shines on something.

solid: A solid has a shape and size.

space: The Earth, moon, sun, and stars are out in space.

star: A star is made of gas and gives off light. The sun is a star.

stem: The stem holds up the plant.

valley: A valley is a low place between mountains or hills.

water: Water is a liquid.

waves: The ocean has waves.

weather: The weather can be sunny or cloudy.

wind: Wind is moving air.

Science Words to Know

Science Skills Test

Circle the correct answers.

1. Which things are alive?

2. Which arrow points to the roots?

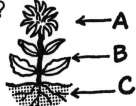

3. Which one comes first?

4. Which animal does not belong in this group?

5. Which animal does not belong in this group?

6. Which bugs are insects?

7. Which animal has fur for a body covering?

8. Which tracks belong to this animal?

9. Which animal belongs in this home?

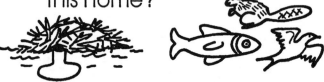

10. Which animal belongs in an ocean habitat?

11. Which bone is the skull?

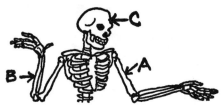

12. Which food is unhealthy?

Name _____

Circle the correct answer or answers.

13. Which plant part makes food?   **roots   stem   leaves**

14. Which plant part makes seeds?   **stem   flower   leaves**

15. A fish is covered with _____.   **scales   fur   feathers**

16. Which animal hops?   **a snake   a fish   a whale   a rabbit**

17. Which body parts can you see?

    tongue   teeth   heart   elbow   lungs

18. Which body system helps you feel things?

    bones   blood   nerves   breathing

19. The Earth moves around the _____.   **moon   sun**

20. The moon moves around the _____.   **sun   Earth**

Match the body parts to the words.

21. ribs

22. ankle

23. brain

24. lungs

25. heart

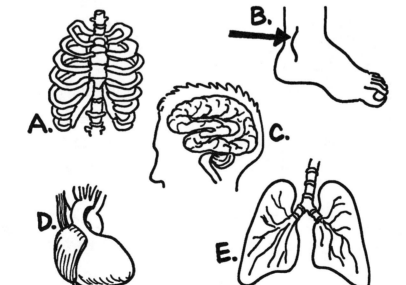

Name _____

Science Skills Test

Circle the correct answers.

26. Which body part is used to hear?

27. Which things are NOT safe?

28. Which one is Earth?

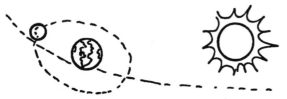

29. Which season is this?

winter **summer**
spring **fall**

30. Which letter is on the part of Earth where it is night?

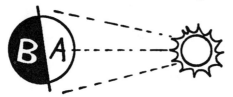

31. Which things are solids?

32. Which things use electricity?

33. Which one of these things is melting?

34. Which things show that air is moving?

35. Which weather is shown here?

windy   **rainy**
sunny   **snowy**

Name _____

60 **Science Skills Test**

Answer Key

Skills Test, pages 58–60

1. bird, flower
2. C
3. 1st picture—roots
4. fish
5. prairie dog
6. ant, ladybug
7. mouse
8. bottom tracks
9. beaver
10. octopus
11. C
12. lollipop
13. leaves
14. flower
15. scales
16. a rabbit
17. tongue, teeth, elbow
18. nerves
19. sun
20. Earth
21. A
22. B
23. C
24. E
25. D
26. ear
27. knife, matches, poison
28. body in center
29. winter
30. B
31. stool, bike
32. toaster, TV
33. ice cube
34. blowing hair, tree
35. rainy

Exercise Pages 10–54

page 10

Living things are—girl, cat, ducks, rat, butterfly, trees, flowers, bushes, grass, mushrooms, flies, cattails

page 11

Things that are not alive are—houses, driveways, bus, balloon, kite, signs, swings, teeter-totter, bench, drinking fountain, stones, buildings, roads, car, skates, pond, toy boat

page 12

Check to see that leaves are light green, stems are dark green, roots are brown, and flowers are other colors.

page 13

1. seeds germinating
2. little plant
3. bud
4. open flower
5. dandelion fluff
6. seeds blowing
7. plant dies

Numbering of pictures on page is 5—3—2—4—1—6—7

page 14

Color 2, 3, 4, 5, 6, 7, 8

page 15

Insects with 6 legs—1, 2, 3, 4, 7, 8, 9, 10, 12
Spiders with 8 legs—5, 11
Centipede with many legs—6

page 16

Bird moves from Reptile Cage to Bird Land

Fish moves from Bird Land to Fish Tank

Cat moves from Fish Tank to Mammal Land

Ostrich moves from Mammal Land to Bird Land

Snake moves from Mammal Land to Reptile Cage

page 17

1. fish—circle in green
2. snail—circle in red
3. frog—circle in yellow
4. ostrich—color
5. bear—circle in blue
6. girl—circle in purple

page 18

1. swim
2. fly
3. climb
4. hop
5. run
6. crawl

page 19

1. dog
2. duck
3. chicken
4. goat
5. rat
6. horse
7. girl

page 20

1. hide
2. make noise
3. sting
4. warn
5. run away

page 21

crocodile to swamp
penguin to iceberg
dog to doghouse
fish to fish bowl
bird to tree
Worm is in the right home—should be colored.

pages 22–23

pond: frog
desert: lizard
forest: squirrel
rain forest: parrot
grassland: elephant, lion
ocean: octopus
arctic: polar bear

page 24

Check to see that students accurately label body parts.

page 25

Check to see that students accurately label body parts.

page 26

1. Circulatory—bleeding
2. Respiratory—blowing up balloon
3. Digestive—eating food

page 27

1. mouth
2. lungs
3. skull
4. knee
5. elbow
6. bones
7. eye

Basic Skills/Science K-1

page 28

1. see
2. taste
3. hear
4. smell
5. feel

page 29

Answers may vary some.

1. see, taste, touch
2. see, hear, touch
3. see, touch
4. see, touch
5. hear
6. touch, see
7. Answers will vary.
8. Answers will vary.

page 30

Healthy foods: broccoli, cherries, oatmeal, fish, bread, carrots, melon, celery, oranges, eggplant, grapes, eggs, milk, cheese

page 31

1. Eat
2. sleep
3. clean
4. day
5. water
6. teeth

page 32

Color: rest, brush teeth, exercise, check-up, good food
There are 5 unhealthy things.

page 33

Put X on: growling dog, matches, sharp scissors
There are 7 healthy things.

page 34

1. sun—yellow

2. moon—purple
3. Earth—blue & green

page 35

1. A
2. B
3. spins

page 36

Examine chart to see that the pictures show things appropriate to the season.

page 37

Check to see that students have colored the four thermometers with the correct temperatures.

page 38

See that pictures are correctly numbered.

page 39

See that student has matched the correct term to the correct picture.

pages 40–41

See that pictures are drawn on the correct spots on the map.

page 42

The coloring will vary.

page 43

1. fish
2. fern
3. frog
4. lizard
5. dinosaur
6. dragonfly

page 44

There may be some variation in answers.

1. gas (possibly solid, also)

Answer Key

2. solid
3. solid, gas
4. liquid
5. solid
6. liquid

page 45

Answers may vary. Discuss these with students.
liquids: water, shampoo, cola
solids: comb, sponge, hose, can, bone, powder, collar, brush, clothes, dog, bubbles, bathtub, Tom, towel

page 46

1. boil
2. bake
3. mix
4. burn
5. expand
6. freeze
7. melt

page 47

Answers will vary.

page 48

1. A
2. D
3. G
4. M
5. Q

page 49

1. yes
2. yes
3. yes
4. yes
5. no
6. no
7. yes

page 50

X on car, cigarette, spray can, smokestack

page 51

Check to see that student's answers are correct.

page 52

location of arrows:
ball kicker—foot
rocket—back end of rocket
swing—arms pushing
weight lifter—arms lifting and/or legs
sled—arms pulling
Circle the big dog.

page 53

1. no
2. no
3. yes
4. no
5. no
6. yes
7. yes
8. no

page 54

Pictures that should be found and outlined in red . . .
lamp
lightbulb
toaster
radio
TV
vacuum cleaner
Pictures that should be found and outlined in blue . . .
toothbrush
glasses
ball
shoe
6 things use electricity